T0195681

A SEASONED
LIFE

GREETING AND HONORING
EACH SEASON AS IT COMES

CHRISTINE MILNER

authorHOUSE®

AuthorHouse™
1663 Liberty Drive
Bloomington, IN 47403
www.authorhouse.com
Phone: 833-262-8899

This book is a work of non-fiction. Unless otherwise noted, the author
and the publisher make no explicit guarantees as to the accuracy of
the information contained in this book and in some cases, names of
people and places have been altered to protect their privacy.

Published by AuthorHouse 10/07/2021

ISBN: 978-1-6655-3787-2 (sc)
ISBN: 978-1-6655-3786-5 (e)

Library of Congress Control Number: 2021918851

Print information available on the last page.

Any people depicted in stock imagery provided by Getty Images are models,
and such images are being used for illustrative purposes only.
Certain stock imagery © Getty Images.

Interior Image Credit: Donna Olson

New American Bible (Revised Edition) (NABRE)
Scripture texts, prefaces, introductions, footnotes and cross references used in this work
are taken from the New American Bible, revised edition © 2010, 1991, 1986, 1970
Confraternity of Christian Doctrine, Inc., Washington, DC All Rights Reserved.

Scripture quotations marked MSG are taken from THE MESSAGE.
Copyright © 1993, 1994, 1995, 1996, 2000, 2001, 2002, 2003 by
Eugene H. Peterson. Used by permission of NavPress Publishing Group.

Scripture quotations marked NKJV are taken from the New King James Version.
Copyright © 1982 by Thomas Nelson, Inc. Used by permission. All rights reserved.

This book is printed on acid-free paper.

Because of the dynamic nature of the Internet, any web addresses or links contained in
this book may have changed since publication and may no longer be valid. The views
expressed in this work are solely those of the author and do not necessarily reflect the
views of the publisher, and the publisher hereby disclaims any responsibility for them.

Contents

About the Author..vii

Dedication ix

Foreword or Preface xi

Ode to the God of the Seasons...........................xvii

Chapter 1   SUMMER: A See-Saw Invitation 1

Chapter 2   AUTUMN: Nothing Lasts Forever 10

Chapter 3   WINTER: The Soul Work of Settling......... 20

Chapter 4   SPRING: Wild and Free...............................29

Afterword 39

About the Author

Christine Milner works and lives in Southbridge, MA. She has been working on writing this book at the urging of many who have participated in workshops and retreats she has given on the topic of Spirituality and the four seasons. She earned a BA in English form Annhurst College, Woodstock, CT, an MA in Religious Studies from Assumption College, Worcester, MA, and a Graduate Certificate in Spirituality from Hartford Seminary, Hartford, CT. She taught English, History, French and Religion for over 20 years in Grades 4 through 12, and courses at Anna Maria College, Paxton, MA, to graduate students in Religious Education. She also served as a Faith Formation Director in a parish for 12 years. In retirement, she remains engaged in retreat work and as a member of the USA Leadership Team of the lay associates of the Sisters of the Assumption, a congregation in which she served as a vowed religious for 7 years and a lay associate for 33 years. She most recently became a Spiritual Director deepening her background by participating in a Supervision group at Holy Cross College, Worcester, MA.

Dedication

To my husband, my champion supporter, our
daughters Sarah, Gereen and Grace, who have caught
the thread and passed it on to Auguste, Elizabeth,
Sigrid, Evelyn and Jameson, our grandchildren.

Foreword or Preface

Acts 17:22....NABRE (New American bible revised edition) translation:

> *He made from one the whole human race*
> *to dwell on the entire surface of the earth,*
> *and he fixed the ordered seasons and the*
> *boundaries of their regions, so that people might*
> *seek God, even perhaps grope for him and find*
> *him, though indeed he is not far from any one*
> *of us*

To ponder that God is the One who fixed the ordered seasons so that humans might seek and grope for this holy Creator is an auspicious thought. To believe that this same God is actually not far from any of us after all is even more so.

While getting ready 20 years ago to celebrate my jubilee [50th] birthday, I thumbed through an assortment of journals I had kept over many years and I found there a palpable "thread" that called to me out of sheer repetition. I could not keep track of how many times in those journals I had expressed through laments, yearnings, poems and songs an obsession-like desire to "have more time" to greet, honor and live in each season as it came. Over those many years I had been a religious, then married and became a wife, mother of three, teacher, master's degree student, parish formation director, lay associate for the Congregation I had belonged to, and grandmother to 5 unbelievable human beings! So I had good reasons I suppose for not always noticing the gifts each season brings, but it's uncanny how many journal entries lamented this fact. I YEARNED for the time to pay more attention! The poems written sometimes years apart scream out the same theme: "oh how my life would be different if only I had more time!"

Welcome to the human condition in this century, right? In those journals I also found an honest and patient seeker though. There are notes and quotes from many books on the subject of "keeping the seasons' so as to grow closer to the God who designed them in the first place. It actually started in the convent where the Psalms were sung morning and evening drilling home that our life on earth is lived in a circular pattern, a dependable rhythm of night followed by day, of Winters followed by Springs and all amidst loss followed by treasure and grief followed by deep joy.

My mother-in-law, Lilian, early on in my marriage, introduced me to Hal Borland and his "Book of Days," a virtual daily diary of what can be discovered when we pay attention. She also gifted me one Christmas with Jean Hersey's "The Shape of a Year," a monthly account of what the author anticipated and experienced one season at a time. Jean, who will never know it, set me on a journey of marking my days from my mid-twenties until now. I still have that book given to me over 40 years ago now, have reread it regularly, and bought one for each of my 3 daughters several Christmases ago. It remains a guide and the author a mentor for what became of my intense yearning.

Sometimes we are given the grace of another soul that understands ours and agrees to journey alongside us. For me, that was my sister-in-law, Sheila. As a farm wife she grasped the coming and going of the seasons better than anyone I knew. The slightest change outside that a new one was upon us would stir excitement inside her, and how she greeted and honored it was to take out a yellow legal pad, of which she had many, and make lists of everything she was going to do to welcome and celebrate that time of year! I caught that practice and spirit and carry it still. She passed away on the very last day of the year appropriately, and that October I spent a week helping her out. It was Full Autumn in Amsterdam, New York!! So, she peeled apples and I rolled out dough for some 30 apple pies that she said she was going to "put by" in her freezer but before the week was out, we had delivered almost all of them to friends and farm neighbors. I learned that however we choose to keep the seasons, the gifts that come to us are always for giving away!

Many years later I reached an age and a time when constraints gave way to freer time and I could finally live out that "thread" that has been there all along, not unlike that elusive God who ends up being so remarkably close after all! Why do I write this book then? To share what I've learned about what honoring the seasons can do for the kind of life that seeks growth in spiritual things, in things that matter.

I write in the hope I can give others a look into what each season can teach us and to suggest ways to greet, honor, embrace, and celebrate each one as it comes.

I stole away to be alone for several days to be able to accomplish this, and so I sit in a tiny cottage on one of the Champlain Islands in Vermont. I owe a tremendous thank you to the owner of these cottages, to which my husband and I have come to each fall for the past five years. There is Wi-fi to which I'm connected, but virtually nothing else, no TV or radio, and I have shut off my cell phone for most of every day. It has been a grace-filled time perfect for reflecting and gathering into a piece countless snippets of talks, retreats, workshops, poems and journal notes that have always begged to one day be a book.

The author of any kind of how-to book should have some experience for the content to ring true. All I offer is a lifetime of yearning, and countless workshops, classes and retreats I've facilitated so often centering [sometimes knowingly often unknowingly] on the thread that is so evident now in the seven decades I have lived. I can say that I have known many rich and wonderful, and quite a few chaotic and painful seasons, and that it took many decades to learn the lessons from both kinds. I'm still learning. I write this book for my daughters, my grandchildren, and anyone with the same yearning to be closer to the One who "set the boundaries" of the four seasons' regions for one reason only, so we could savor each one. The Masai have in their catechism the question, "Why did God create the earth?" The answer is poignant: "Because he thought we might enjoy it!"

God saw that it was very good for human beings to experience four changing and diverse seasons to every year they lived on this planet. It is a dependable and faithful rhythm that not one of us can alter. We cannot predict when one season ends and another begins, nor can we make them come any sooner if we wanted to. Each one can be a gift. The kind that comes unexpectedly and usually at just the right time. It took too many missed seasons, too many years of being so busy as to not even enjoy one before another was already upon me. But all along, a voice inside was persistent: "make time" …. "THIS Spring is important; it won't ever come again!" …. "What can I do to savor THIS season?" …. "Make time!!"

All that is really required is a willingness to pay attention, to observe and notice the subtle changes as one season diminishes and another crawls in. Annie Dillard comes to mind… "The answer must be, I think, that beauty and grace are performed whether or not we will or sense them. The least we can do is try to be there."

My hope is that you have figured out how to do this in the midst of the hurried and busy life we all seem to be living these days, and that it didn't take you as long as it did for me. If that is the case perhaps these pages can affirm what you yourself have already come to know. If you're still yearning, I can hope that these pages encourage you that living a season-ed life turns out to be pretty simple. Just as adding just the right spice or herb to a dish can completely transform it, so too will "keeping" the seasons add a rich dimension to your life!

In the following chapters, one for each of the four seasons, I pass on some of the ways Summer, Autumn, Winter and Spring can grow our spiritual side and lead us to live more wholehearted, "seasoned" lives. As I myself have learned to show up and "be there," a very sweet image has come to me of how these seasons have their way of coming to us as gifts from the One who simply wants us to enjoy them. For me, each one descends upon us like a shawl right from the hands of our good God. In each shawl, She has woven in the dependable, cherished gifts and lessons of that specific season. These 4 shawls never fail to nourish and sustain us, to fill us with an abundance of good things.

Each season invites you to smell its scents and see its beauties as you live and dance--- laugh and cry through its weeks, until a new shawl descends upon your shoulders.

When I shared this image with an artist friend of mine, she graciously and beautifully illustrated the concept for me, which you see as the cover of the book and the template that introduces each chapter. Thank you, Donna, for all the love in those sketches.

A word about my husband of 46 years. A man with a strong work ethic and farm background was perfectly suited for this small mill town girl yearning for a closer connection with the land in all its seasons. Over the years he has taught me much especially about God's main role in humans' lives: to be a source of strength. While some turn to familiar rote prayers in times of trouble or seek holy places of comfort, my husband gets on a tractor and in solitude plows, tills or harvests row after circular row till the cows come home. Grief and loss are reckoned with through the repetitive, soothing sound of a tractor out in a field for however long it takes. There he finds God, a sense of balance, and an assurance he is never alone. That has been a powerful lesson for me, and for that and so much love and devotion, thank you, Clyde. You are constantly reflected in the four chapters that follow.

Ode to the God of the Seasons

i want to learn from the expert Weaver
how to tie the threads together
of a lifetime lived
stained, stamped and storied by four
four ever changing spans meant to shape me four ways to meet
the Weaver head-on
to kneel, to taste, to "keep"
i have laughed and cried through the four
ever mourning for not enough time
yet You never stopped did You?
through all my years each of the four came
one at a time...unbidden...sometimes unnoticed... grace like
spilled water seeping in
wrapping me round...in a rhythm I can count on ever ancient,
ever new, ever four

~Cmilner

Chapter One

SUMMER: A See-Saw Invitation

Gladys Taber, another mentor of mine for navigating the seasons, once wrote, "As long as you have a window, life is exciting." I had to decide which season I would begin with in this glimpse at all four, and I landed on summer because it's the one during which I'm always at my window looking out to make sure it's still here. It's a season, here in New England especially that has a timing all its own never beginning at the same time each year. It's also the season I find hardest to let go of when signs point unmistakably to its demise. I pass by any window in my home and cannot stop myself from looking out not wanting to miss a single new blossom, or I might just catch a mama raccoon at the edge of my woods urging her cubs to follow her out of the yard, except they're too busy tumbling over empty pots left on my planting table. If summer is about anything, it is about taking the time to "take it all in," It is about abundance, fruitfulness, fulfilled promises! I have come to know summer as a series of endless infinitives; a time for playing, vacationing, enjoying a hammock, eating ice cream, picking fresh vegetables, canning, hiking, driving away, driving back. A season that can easily deceive you into thinking it's going to last forever. The calendar sets the boundaries of summer as June 20 to September 20, but this season has a mind of its own. Due to the fact I was a teacher for many years, a strong association set summer for me as starting on the last day of school in June and ending on the last days in August when we returned to our classrooms. Since leaving that world, more days and weeks were restored to me in which to savor the true gifts of summer: the early rising of the sun and its late setting all but scream to us the spirit of this season, "Life is meant to be lived fully and abundantly!!"

It's a time to experience new places...new people....it is a time to cultivate and water what you planted in Spring.... AND to weed out what shouldn't be there!! The analogies to our spirit lives are obvious and plentiful....it is time to ripen...... and to clothe yourself with the fruits of the Spirit: joy, peace, patience, kindness......

Liturgically in many faith traditions, summer is Ordinary Time!!! But the profusion we see out there when we look out our windows is anything but ordinary. Colors abound with green topping the list followed closely by purples, blues and yellows. Actually, no time is ordinary for those with eyes to see: as one author puts it, "summer reminds us of the insane generosity of God." I'm reminded of the summers of France and Belgium, with their alternating fields of sunflowers and lavender, that inspired St Julie Billiard---foundress of the Sisters of Notre Dame--- to exclaim "Ah, qu'il est bon, le bon Dieu!" "OH, but our God is so good!!" It became the community's mantra.

So what are some ways to greet and honor the season of summer, to celebrate its distinct colors, gifts, and to balance its see-saw invitations to rest and reflect at the same time as engage in activity galore? The ways I practice that enable me to be more present to every changing season will involve such varied things as prayer, decorating, to just generally engaging in actions that reflect that season. Reading what others have said about summer for example, or poems people have written get us in touch with a different lens that we don't always use. Sing songs that scream summer. Cook a meal that is quintessential summer.

The good God of summer beckons us to waste time with the divine....to make use of the looser schedule/the slower rhythm that the heat necessitates...to practice summer spirituality: picnics, lingering at meals, sitting and gazing...... going for what the Spirituality and Practice website posted as a way to grow in spirituality in the summertime: a walk "for the glory of God..." Walking with attention praying something like, " I walk in the midst of your creation, God, with eyes wide open and I give you praise for the glory that surrounds me." When you pray in the season of summer, speak summer names for God in moments of resting and savoring!! Names like "Sparkling Mystery," "Bringer of Sunshine," "Sweet Giver of gifts," "Giver of Sun and Rain."

Another suggestion is to go barefoot....becoming aware of what the grass, and the earth really feel like without shoes.... again...we are reminded that decades ago, folks were outside in all seasons....they experienced seeing, smelling and feeling a thunderstorm coming on...letting ourselves do that connects us to a former way of life, one that connected us with the rest of creation. Smell the rain before it comes and go outside when it's pouring out and let yourself get totally drenched.........no running for shelter and becoming exasperated because you're soaked.........this provides a dimension that all of us have lost in the present age we live in....a dimension GOOD for our souls!!!

Another summer practice is actually one I will suggest to use each season to grow spiritually...In your prayer space.... [and if you don't have one, I invite you to create one!] It can be a porch rocker, a corner of a room carved out by you or a garden bench; a personal space to retreat to daily to just be] in summer you could bring golden objects that help you honor the Sun....Use your iphone to take pictures of what you see as you walk in each summer...display these in the place you go to be alone and to think of things that matter....think outside the box....a photo of a child eating ice cream, sunrise or sunset you happened to capture on vacation, a neighbor finally getting to take a nap in his hammock.

I have long had the practice of seizing a summer afternoon to sit and write a story of what the year has been so far... sometimes I refer to it when sending a newsy Christmas greeting to friends far away. I call it "summer-izing." As you will see in the Winter chapter, I journal on the last day of every year: encapsulating this "summer-y" along with what I've seen and experienced in the last 4 months not yet written down. I express gratitude for each person—old and new—that has graced the living of that year, and then to greet the new year that begins the next day I jot down hopes and dreams for what lies ahead. I make it a practice to 'check' on those hopes and dreams every now and then to get a sense that I'm following the path I laid out for myself, or notice and take stock of how maybe the Spirit had other ideas!

A truth about summer is that it doesn't last forever..it never does. As much as I struggle each year to let it go, doing so never fails to drive home once more a spiritual truth: when you remain wrapped up in what you have lost, there is no room to embrace what is yet to come. Put your arms solidly around each summer, enjoy, drink it all in. But then if you find it hard, like me, to say goodbye allow yourself time to slowly release its gifts and open your heart and mind to the new Season just around the corner. Summer will return again, whether we are here to greet her or not. You can count on that!

I end this chapter as I will end them all: encouraging readers to look up and cherish certain poems, and listen/dance to particular songs that capture the essence of that season. I also will end each chapter with simple creative décor ideas that facilitate greeting and honoring it as it comes, and personal, family recipes that celebrate its gifts and bounty.

Christine Milner

<u>Summer Poems</u>: (I urge my readers to look up and savor these poems in their entirety…)

From Blossoms by —*Li-Young Lee*
From blossoms comes
this brown paper bag of peaches
we bought from the boy
at the bend in the road where we turned toward
signs painted Peaches………………………….

Summer Stars by —*Carl Sandburg*
Bend low again, night of summer stars.
So near you are, sky of summer stars,
So near, a long arm man can pick off stars,
Pick off what he wants in the sky bowl,……………………………

<u>A Summer Song:</u> **Today**—*written by Randy Sparks —sung by John Denver*

(Give yourself a summer treat and play this entire song!)

Today, while the blossoms still cling to the vine
I'll taste your strawberries, I'll drink your sweet wine
A million tomorrows shall all pass away
'Ere I forget all the joy that is mine, today..................................

last day of August

the sound of that just stings
innocent goldenrod still triggers thoughts of new notebooks and
the start of the school year
though I haven't taught for many years nor been a student many
more
not a fan of letting summer go
i scheme for one more beach day
one more nearly 9:00 sunset
yet I somehow manage slowly
to watch as it slips away
september gets ahold of me and off I go to gather goldenrod and
wait until it finds its place
among gourds and sunflowers
and I find mine as I snuggle into autumn

~Cmilner

Greeting summer with décor:

I've alluded already to creating a prayer space in your home and to honor summer by placing in it one or two "objects" that say summer to YOU! iPhone photos of something endearing that you notice or experience while this season lingers is another way. Your front door, your yard if you have one, the kitchen and/or dining room table are all spots that can witness that in this house lives someone who celebrates each season simply and well. Changing out house flags, a simple sailboat under a glass cloche, a sign that reads, "Hello, Summer!" All are ways to encourage living in the flow and rhythm of the season we are in right NOW. It does not have to cost very much at all if anything. What it requires is showing up…being there to welcome summer, in this case, each time it rolls around. What this creates is a closeness to the One who created the beauty of a Sunday afternoon in June and the first corn on the cob of July. What this generates is a rich life lived to the full.

Summer Recipes:

A farmer's wife and good friend served us this keeper on a warm summer weekend trip to her upstate NY farm. Making it always brings me back there…

Barbara Taylor's Baked Beans

[Many years ago, a few of us traveled by motorcycle to visit some farming friends of ours who had moved up to upstate New York. We arrived early in the evening and we were treated to a hot dogs and beans casserole, which our hostess said was her own creation! It was so delicious we asked for her recipe which has now been passed on lovingly to the next generation and affectionately called **Barbara Taylor's Baked Beans.***]*

Ingredients:

4-5 slices of bacon, cut up
1 small onion (sliced)
¾ cup brown sugar
1 cup catsup
1 TBlsp yellow mustard
1 TBlsp vinegar
1 lb kielbasa (sliced)

Directions:

Sauté the bacon pieces with the onion and add the remaining sauce ingredients. Pour into a slow cooker and add the kielbasa slices plus 1 can each pork & beans/drained kidney beans/drained butter beans. Cook on low 5-6 hours. You can also pour it all in a casserole dish and bake at 350 for one hour.

A Scriptural Picnic

This delightful "recipe" was born one summer day when a Sister friend of mine was visiting and we brought my 3 toddler daughters to the lake. Sister Anne suggested we pack up a Scriptural picnic, which she claimed consisted of a freshly baked French bread, a bottle of wine [which that day was a bottle of grape juice…], and an 8-ounce wedge of sharp cheddar cheese! A tradition was born…

Chapter Two

AUTUMN: Nothing Lasts Forever

I'm not a goodbye girl!! The day I surrender to saying goodbye to summer, behold I come face to face with a season whose other name is weighed down with more surrender, letting go and impermanence: FALL!! All around us depending on where you live there may very well be an explosion of fiery oranges and golds, but those leaves are also falling away one by one. Listen to what some of my mentors have to say about this season:

"September is a sweep of dusky, purple asters, a sumac branch swinging a fringe of scarlet leaves, and the bittersweet scene of wild grapes when I walk down the lane to the mailbox. September is a golden month of mellow sunlight and still clear days. ... Small creatures in the grass, as if realizing their days are numbered, cram the night air with sound. Everywhere goldenrod is full out." *Jean Hersey*

"Indian summer comes gently, folds over the hills and valleys as softly as the fall of a leaf on a windless day. It is always unexpected. After a sharp cold spell, we wake one morning and look out and the very air is golden. The sky has a delicate dreamy color, and the yet unfallen leaves on the bravest trees have a secure look, as if they would never, never fall." *Gladys Taber*

"Autumn is the eternal corrective. It is ripeness and color and a time of maturity; but it is also breadth, and depth, and distance. What man can stand with autumn on a hilltop and fail to see the span of his world and the meaning of the rolling hills that reach to the far horizon?" *Hal Borland*

> **Please also reference** *FALL SONG, by Mary*
> *Oliver, and relish the whole of it!*
> *Another year gone, leaving everywhere*
> *its rich spiced residues: vines, leaves,*
> *the uneaten fruits crumbling damply*
> *in the shadows, unmattering back*

Other's voices can and do give us a different lens through which we see more clearly and understand a bit more, something like the coming of fall, that you have witnessed repeatedly. Each season to me offers at least 2 distinctive points of view, and Autumn ranks high in that category.

It can be an exhilarating season and a melancholy one all at the same time. In the Spring we have planted and cultivated, all Summer we have weeded and watered, and now in Autumn all our labor comes into its own. It is an experience of full maturity....it is easy to see why it is associated with the spiritual season of middle age plus....All around us outside there is a visible tension.....letting go and storing away....dying and diminishment but also wild gold and oranges!

As the leaves tumble down, our spirits ask: "what do I need to release.... how can I get out of my own way and let Spirit take charge?" The lesson of autumn is that everything is impermanent... nothing lasts forever.....at any chronological age, this season is an invitation from God to take inventory....where have I been?... what have I learned? What am I harvesting and for whom? What will I pass on to another generation? As women especially, I believe, we have the responsibility to engage our daughters and granddaughters' imaginations to see what really matters in life [in fact add on nieces and neighbors' daughters]. Who will stir up these imaginings within them with a passion for God's Spirit if we do not? Listen to one of my favorite poems encompassing all the seasons, written by Franciscan Sister Patricia Anne Mulkey, OSF:

SEASON OF THE OAKS

In the Winter the crisp, brown leaves tenaciously hold fast
    to their mother tree above,
singing, lamenting like Jeremiah, naked in the wind.

In the Spring these old ones watch new-green buds
    crowd their branches;

some pushed off, leaping to the ground,
    but others stay.

In the Summer these persistent brown, crusty ones
    live in the luscious green canopy.
        Their crispy old voices
            Chattering to their friends.

Autumn Frost brings the message of rest for the gold,
    red and brown acrobats
        who tumble to the ground,
            again becoming soil,
                but not the ones with staying power.

They will hold fast:
    Or who will show the young spring things
        How to dance,
        How to hold fast in storms,
        How to sing the tree-songs,
How to bend and shine with syncopated rain,
Or how to make the musky fragrances?

They dream and remember a future, a gospel of how things
should be.
They dance artfully and recall a Druid's breath.

Every September I experience the same deep reluctance to
let go of summer; I resist and don't want it to die.... but here
the tension between 2 seeming opposites again: it's the end of
carefree-ness and hello to a new school year, new adventures....
the idea of beginning again is as palpable as it is in Spring!!!!
My thoughts linger on my reluctance to face my own death
during this season.....to have to separate from cherished ones....

the thought of never again seeing a sunrise.... at least on this side of life.... the notion that there will come a time when I will no longer be here..... Letting go and trusting is perhaps the hardest thing for human beings to do.......One of my favorite Sufi parables is the one about the journeying stream. You might be familiar with the story that follows a little stream from its source high in the mountains describing all its meanderings through diverse countryside barriers until it reaches desert sand. It finds after several attempts that it simply cannot get through without completely being absorbed by the hot sands and it does not want to lose its individuality and disappear. It suddenly hears a voice that explains it must let the wind swallow it up and let itself be carried over the desert by the wind. The little stream very much doubts that it will work, and it has never been completely absorbed by anything before. Here the stream echoes familiar human emotion and doubt concerning our death by asking "How does this happen...and how can I be sure that I will become a stream again?" The voice tells the stream that the wind carries its essence over the desert and drops it back down as rain where it gathers strength and flows freely again. It finally lifts its vapor into the arms of the wind and is safely deposited as rain on the other side. How closely this parable describes the trust we must have when it comes time to fall like the leaves in autumn and allow ourselves to be transformed "on the other side."

Each autumn, I have to relearn that goodbyes are part of life.... ending and closures are sad...but this season teaches that they are also very necessary...like darkness is necessary to see the stars.

If I want to grow spiritually during Autumn, I must find time to reckon, settle, bring things to a conclusion, perhaps bring in wood, lay up for the coming winter, can tomatoes.... I need to grow and I need to grow up....mature... and celebrate the mysteries of life!! In fact, during this season like no other, you and I encounter Mystery.........we will never know all there is to know about God in this life...and it will take all of eternity to discover it in the next! You and I, in autumn, catch glimpses of the God who takes away and fills us... all with the same Hand. What do we do with Mystery???? We embrace it...we are humbled before It... we are grateful to be part of It......... we let it be!! We might call on God during these months with Autumn names like, "Wordless Rhapsody," "Faithful One," and "Artist of Life."

It's no accident that during this season we gather.... we give thanks.....and we humbly ask God to make us open to whatever awaits us...and the grace to live life to the fullest! It is a time to bring to a prayer space a leaf, an apple, a pumpkin, a goose feather, a warm sweater: symbols to remind me of the gifts of autumn. Take part in harvesting if you can during these months, attend festivals and fairs, be sure to spend as much time as you can OUTSIDE where your senses will remember the tastes, smells and sights of this plentiful and abundant season. Do not be afraid to feel the melancholy that so easily comes as leaves let go and fall but look at the "dying" as a dance of what we have known and what we have yet to know. Look around you and do not miss the weeks of exhilarating, wild colors. If the earth we have known can be this glorious, what awaits us? For those who believe, what awaits us will be indescribable!!

Christine Milner

AUTUMN POEMS

An Autumn poem written many years ago when I was still yearning for more time to "notice":

I just decided today that fall has come;
Oh, I had noticed the golds and browns before now,
But something in the way the leaves
fell this afternoon
spoke to me of a summer that is past
and a crisp chill son to take control.
I wonder why it came to me this way—
Maybe I ought to open my door
Wider
and take the seasons by the
hand just a wee bit tighter
than I have up to now.
Something in the way I live....

~Cmilner

AUTUMN SONG

"Come, Ye Thankful People, Come"

Come, ye thankful people, come,
Raise the song of harvest home!
All is safely gathered in,
Ere the winter storms begin;
—*Henry Alford [based on Psalm 100:4]*

GREETING AUTUMN WITH DÉCOR:

I have already mentioned possibilities for lacing certain visuals in a prayer space above; when looking to greet this season at your front door and in your yard, try to think creatively to avoid getting bored with the customary pumpkins and scarecrows. No need to throw away what you've used before…to be frugal simply place what was at your front steps somewhere else this year……try a splash of a new fall color, like teal, or bald and white, among your orange gourds and pumpkins! One year, instead of placing a scarecrow I had in a front circular garden each year, I decided to place him behind a shrub in such a way as he looked like he was peeking behind it. Set up an autumn picnic scene with dolls or teddy bears somewhere in your yard…. the falling leaves will add to your design daily at no cost! The sailboat you may have placed under a glass cloche in Summer, can simply be replaced with a string of lights and perhaps some walnuts and a ceramic bird. Pick leaves with vibrant colors before they wither, wrap them in Saran, then foil, and freeze them to use on your Thanksgiving table!

Watch attentively for signs that summer is giving way to this new season so as to greet and honor Autumn when it arrives…not in July like so many department stores, but around mid-September when surely you will smell and feel it.

AUTUMN RECIPES

[Although there must be hundreds of variations on this classic fall dessert, here is my favorite, inspired by a local family orchard.]

APPLE CRISP

Ingredients & Directions:

5 cups apples, sliced
¾ cup sugar
½ tsp cinnamon
½ cup hot water
1 TBlsp butter

Slice apples into a pan 9 "square; add mixed sugar & cinnamon. Dot with butter. Add hot water, cover pan tightly with foil and let simmer over very low heat while preparing crusty layer:

1 cup sugar
1 cup flour
1 tsp baking powder
½ tsp salt
2 TBlsp butter
1 egg

Mix dry ingredients, cut in butter, add beaten egg, and mix well. Finish mixing with fingers, then drop pieces of stiff batter onto the boiling hot apples, spreading it to make a layer. Bake, uncovered in a 350 oven, for 40 minutes or until the brown, crusty layer is done. Serve hot or cold. 9 servings

SLOW-COOKER "DON'T TELL THE NEIGHBORS" BEEF STEW

[This recipe is from my brother-in-law Stuart who assured me that neighbors will come with empty bowls as soon as they detect the aroma of your cooking it...]

2 lbs stew beef
¼ cup flour1 ½ tsp salt
½ tsp pepper

Cut meat into bite-size pieces and place in bottom of slow cooker. Combine flour, salt and pepper and sprinkle over, then toss to coat meat well. Add 1 ½ cups beef broth, and 1 tsp. Worcestershire sauce, garlic salt to taste, 1 bay leaf, and 1 tsp paprika. Add 4 sliced carrots, 3 large potatoes, diced and slices of turnip or parsnip, whatever you have on hand. Mix well and cover and cook on low for 10-12 hours or on high for 4-6 hours.

Chapter Three

WINTER: The Soul Work of Settling

"The hush comes with the deepening of Autumn; but it comes gradually. Our ears are attuned to it, day by quieter day. But even now, if one awakens in the deep darkness of the small hours, one can hear it, a foretaste of Winter silence. It's a little painful now, and a little lonely because it is so strange."—*Hal Borland*

"January is the month for dreaming." —*Jean Hersey*

"It is winter proper; the cold weather, such as it is, has come to stay. I bloom indoors in the winter like a forced forsythia; I come in to come out." —*Annie Dillard*

If you live as I do in a northern clime, you will most likely come across two vastly different kinds of people when it comes to the winter season: some hate the thought of it and many of these head south to escape it. Others welcome winter with open arms either because they understand its necessity and the gifts it brings, or are motivated by their love of skiing, or skating or snowshoeing! There may very well be folks in between these two poles somewhere as well.

Winter for me takes getting used to, but once I've accepted it and greeted it properly, I settle in for "my long winter's nap." Settling is an appropriate activity for this season of cold, seeming barrenness, and darkness. It is THE season where if I do the "work" it calls me to, I will be able to grow, arms and heart wide open, to receive the seasons to come.

Winter, like all the other seasons, can be a mirror reflecting my own inner changes and rhythms....my own hopes and desires. When this inner chemistry is in line with what is occurring outside of me in nature.... I am in balance....I learn.....I grow!

Outside, it is largely a silent world and everywhere seems to be the invitation to let go.... burrow...it is a season to hibernate, plunge down, reflect, lie fallow. Trees are bare, the landscape stark and barren.....how do I respond to what seemingly is a total lack of anything truly alive!!??

We know of course that there is actually teeming life and activity deep inside the earth....it is simply hidden from us for a time...spiritually speaking then, what am I being called to do...to be during this season? For one thing, I can look for spiritual teachers in this season: trudging through snow creates your very own path that was not there before.... a path Thomas Merton compared to the spiritual life. Frost can also be a teacher, advising that we notice, pay attention, show up and let what we see teach us! Joyce Rupp has meditated on the window frost she once observed and how it taught her to not underestimate the deadness of winter: "all the time we thought we were dead inside, beautiful things were being born in us."

Winter is a gift!!! A virtual invitation to attune myself to and join in with what the rest of creation seems to be about: it's a season to go for a long walk with myself....with no ipad/no iphone/no distractions....and as I notice what's going on in nature ask myself, "what do I need to let go of...or let fall away from my life so I can grow closer to the holiness of God?"

Winter is a season to journal what I desire God to transform within me, like the Creative-Spirit God is transforming all around me in a silent, hidden way. If I mimic what's going on outside, put away all the Christmas décor, and instead keep the winter ambience in my inside home simple, uncluttered and clean, I am reclaiming the practices of the ancients who,, for example in winter would bring in evergreen branches into their homes, and gathered around fires at their own inside hearths and bonfires outside to encourage the sun to shine more brightly during the short, dark days. It is true that our ancestors were so much more tuned in to the natural rhythms of life around them as wanderers spending most of their time outdoors, then for centuries as farmers so at one with the land and at the mercy of the vagaries of the changing seasons. Largely, in the 21st century, we are not outdoors nearly as much as the ancient ones, and sadly have lost that deep connection with the earth and its rhythms!

Winter has its own spirituality however and it IS possible to recover some of that closeness to nature by cultivating a desire for and a practice of solitude, meditation, simplicity, and the virtue of WAITING!! This season invites us all to do just that.

At my prayer time during this season, I could expand on the way I address God with names that flow naturally with what is going on all around me...names like, "Defender of the deep down hidden things," "Brooding Spirit," "Perspective Giver," and "Nurturing One." [Joyce Rupp: "Fragments of Your Ancient Name"]

If in your faith tradition, you celebrate Christmas it is no accident that it occurs a mere 4 days after the winter solstice. The mystery of the Incarnation speaks powerfully of the Son of God "letting go" of his divinity to be able to grow into the fullness of humanity. Jesus literally plunged down and burrowed into our humanity and allowed his status as God's son to lie fallow for a while...

And toward the end of winter the Christian faith gives us the gift of Lent where yearly I'm invited to ask for a cleaner heart and clearer eyes to see. These are not accidents but a Wise Spirit guiding us to flow with what is going on around us in the created world.

We shouldn't hibernate just to escape the cold and dark of winter though. The ancient spiritual masters warn of the temptation to retreat to get away from worldly realities; we let ourselves lie fallow during winter only to become more productive and fruitful later on. We burrow in order to have more to give. We replenish our wells so that we can quench others' thirsts. And so I plunge down in winter to take inventory and warm myself by the fire, to rest, to think.... Spring is coming!!! And there will be much to do!!

Christine Milner

WINTER POEMS

Look up and enjoy all of "Talking in Their Sleep" —*Edith M. Thomas*

"You think I am dead," The apple tree said,
"Because I have never a leaf to show- Because I stoop,
And my branches droop,
And the dull gray mosses over me grow!"

I absolutely love, "To Winter" in its entirety —*Claude McKay*

Stay, season of calm love and soulful snows!
There is a subtle sweetness in the sun,
I read these pregnant signs, know what they mean:
I know that thou art making ready to go......"

And of course don't forget "To Know The Dark" —*Wendell Berry*

To go in the dark with a light is to know the light.
To know the dark, go dark. Go without sight,
and find that the dark, too, blooms and sings,
and is traveled by dark feet and dark wing

WINTER SONGS

Take the time to listen to all the lyrics of the following songs:

"Winter Time" —*Steve Miller Band [Hear it as winter "calling" out her invitation]*
In the winter time When all the leaves are brown
And the wind blows so chill
And the birds have all flown for the summer
I'm callin', hear me callin', hear me callin'..........................

"Winter Snow" —*Chris Tomlin*
Could've come like a mighty storm
With all the strength of a hurricane
You could've come like a forest fire
With the power of Heaven in Your flame......................

GREETING WINTER WITH DÉCOR:

The key in honoring this season lies in reflecting what is happening in nature during these months, so think minimally, thin-ly, bare-ly, and simply. Some ideas would be a few birch branches tucked here and there, white stones/ pinecones/ and a small white candle under a glass dome, create a tiny winter scene inside a lantern, or a simple grapevine wreath with one artificial pine tree and a few snowflakes at your front door. What we see visually affirms what we desire in our hearts: we've "put away" the flowers of summer, the pumpkins of autumn, and we strip down, lie fallow for a while waiting for the burst of new life which is just around the corner.

WINTER RECIPES

Mémère Gravel's Tourtière:

[A 5th generation Canadian recipe, it is traditionally Served on Christmas Eve; my oldest grandson has now had the recipe handed down to him]

Ingredients

2 lbs ground beef/1 lb ground pork
3 potatoes, peeled, sliced and boiled/mash when cool
1 cup diced onion & celery
Seasonings to taste: salt & pepper/cinnamon/cloves/sage, parsley, poultry seasoning

Directions

Sauté the onion and celery in a bit of olive oil. Add the ground beef and pork and cook until meat is no longer pink. Drain, but not completely. Ad the mashed potatoes and season with salt, pepper, cinnamon, cloves, and parsley. [You may have to adjust with a bit more cinnamon according to your taste preference.] Be more liberal with the sage and poultry seasoning until the mixture is to your liking. [Our family prefers a stronger taste of sage & poultry seasoning, but tastebuds vary.] Use your favorite pie crust recipe. Ladle the meat mixture into a pastry lined deep dish pie plate, and cover with a top crust, seal and flute. Bake at 375 degrees for 30 -40 minutes.

Coffee Butterball Cookies:

[This recipe was taken from the label of a Maxwell House Instant coffee jar years ago...]

Ingredients

¾ cup butter
1/3 cup confectioners' sugar
1 ½ TBLSP instant coffee
½ tsp baking soda
1 TBLSP water
1 tsp vanilla 1 ¾ cups flour
1 cup finely chopped nuts

Directions

Cream butter and add the confectioner's sugar. Continue to cream until fluffy. Dissolve instant coffee and baking soda in the water; add to butter mixture with vanilla. Beat well. Stir in flour and nuts. Shape into small balls. Bake on ungreased baking sheet at 350 degrees for 15-18 minutes. Roll each cookie in additional confectioners' sugar while still hot. Makes about 3 dozen.

Chapter Four

SPRING: Wild and Free

In Jean Hersey's book, "The Shape of a Year," she shares a delightful anecdote about a little girl who is visiting her elderly neighbor. The little one complains about how long winter and its cold and darkness have lasted this year! She asks the elder woman, "Do you think Spring will ever come this year?" The wise old soul continues rocking and knitting and without even lifting her head answers, "Always does!!"

In those two words, the little girl hears a lifetime of experience and an affirmation that God has set these seasons; they **always** come, and they always go in a dependable flow and rhythm that we are wise to slide into.

Spring is that season we yearn for that takes its sweet time arriving, but when it does it is unmistakable. The thing about Spring is it awakens in some of us this urgency to clean up, rake, fertilize, plant, and feverishly go about getting "spring chores" done. It's a good urgency as it gets us outside and paying attention! But that urgency can also rob us of things we will not see or hear or sense because we're in a frenzy to get things done! I always feel like I've waited so very long that I must go outside and don't want to miss a thing. Thank goodness for a tiny voice that stops me in my tracks by helping me remember that unless I SIT, unless I'm out there sometimes doing nothing, I'm sure to miss a lot! Here's a Mary Oliver poem about just that for you to look up and enjoy on one of the first mornings you "notice" that Spring has come! Read it through more than once!

"Such Singing in the Wild Branches" ```*Mary Oliver*

> It was spring
> and I finally heard him
> among the first leaves––
> then I saw him clutching the limb.............

As her poem comes to a close, she plants an urgency inside you to get out there before you miss even one thing!

I do admit it is difficult to slow down in Spring; everything seems to be shouting reminders of things you don't want to forget. "Don't forget to clean out the birdhouses so the sparrows return," "Don't forget to prune the butterfly bush, to lime the lawn, to "open" the screened porch, to plant the lettuce early." The list seems endless but after our "long winter's nap," we simply need to remember to slow down; it will all get done in due time. Take time to smell what springs smells like after a brief shower, to watch the columbine return in the garden, and for me, the flowering almond my mother-in-law planted when she was a little girl giving each of her daughters and daughters in law a tiny cutting, which is now an 80 some odd years old, full out shrub I need to prune each year! Give yourself the gift of that first morning when you go outside, and you just simply can't believe it!! It's Spring!! Have you ever not been surprised by spring?

I mean logically we all know it's coming....it always does!!! Yet it always seems to catch us off guard.... even if you've been trying to pay attention to the subtle changes....when did those maple buds get fatter??? when did the cardinal start up his spring tune?....when did the earth soften and send up its sweet, loamy scent?

Spring teaches us humility......humans did not invent the turning of the seasons.... certainly not the gloriousness of Spring....we cannot make it happen sooner...nor can we stop it from coming.... we cannot control Uncontrollable Spring!!! But we were created to receive it....it seems to me that what is important to this season is our response....as people in touch with God's Spirit at the very least our hearts should quicken.... and our arms fling wildly in awe and bewilderment!!! It's no accident ONCE AGAIN... that Christians celebrate the

Resurrection during this season.... the liturgical powers that be say "no Easter Vigil before the first full moon after the vernal equinox!!" Only as we taste the wonder of spring can we dare to rejoice in Jesus' victory over death/Winter??!

If winter was all about BEING...burrowing deep within.... Spring is all about BECOMING...flinging open the windows.... breathing in fresh, crisp, clean air. Spiritual practices that very naturally correspond to this season are artistic, creative endeavors. Tis the season to spring into action.......to create the unique expression of yourself!! Our culture---the world we live in today--- kills creativity.... from toddlers to about 6 years of age we readily claim to be creative.....................if you've ever walked into a classroom of little ones and asked, "I need volunteer painters.... who here is a good painter??" Easily, 15 hands fly up.... try that in an 8th grade room....an assembly of adults??? At 2 - 6 years old, we easily break into song.... move to the beat of music.... but after 6 this gradually but definitely gets silenced. Why????

What gets cut first in public funding for education: the arts!! Time to practice creativity is all but gone in our schools, in our government....in our sanctuaries!! Our only hope is to relearn the natural rhythm of Spring......bring what is going on outside into your home...

Spring is the season to plant, decorate, paint, freshen up, create beauty to mimic the abundance of Beautiful outside!! Something is in the air.............the gusty cold wind becomes a caressing gentle breeze.........the birds can't shut up.... they must sing!!!!! It's with urgency that they gather.... build nests.... give birth. Our Spirit grows during this season.... BUT only in the measure in which you and I also sing, build our nests, give birth to something!!

If you have a garden whether it is a tiny bit of a thing or a far-flung English wildflower one, and you love to be IN it, you are a person who has come to understand the gift of Spring. Gardening, Thomas Berry says, "is an active participation in the deepest mysteries of the universe." "Nearer to God in a garden than any other place on earth...." WHY??? Because it connects you to the passing of time, the source of our food and beauty! I must have 20 pair of gardening gloves.... but Spring approaches and I buy a new pair in a vibrant color. Now that my daughters are grown, their yearly "Easter basket" prominently features a new pair too....and they look forward to seeing them!! Pinterest had a pin not long ago about what to do with old gardening gloves!!! I have all I need for that DIY project!!

Our spirituality must be grounded in the everyday!!! To grow in our life with God we must notice the changes occurring in the outer world, change our steps in unison with these changes, and bring them into our dwelling places! When at prayer, call on God with Spring names: like "O Constant One," "Uncontainable Love," "Midwife of the Soul," "Sweet Presence."

A Spring spirituality practice would be to place a vase of pussy willows on your table.... with intention...or to buy a bunch of daffodils and hand them out randomly at drive-up windows...in parking lots.... it's risky....... you will get shocked looks, awkwardness, and wide, genuine smiles... it's called Incarnational living! You'll love this experience!!! And you'll never know what it causes...................What is it that Mother Theresa said? "Kind words can be short and easy to speak, but their echoes are truly endless." And so besides prettying up your table, you get pussy willows for someone who can't go pick her own anymore; you hand out daffodils with a kind word or smile...You pay for the person in back of you at the Dunkin Donuts drive thru. IT'S SPRING!!!!!

Christine Milner

SPRING calls to us every year to immerse ourselves in the abundance of beautiful around us: listen to a piece of beautiful music, visit a museum, and get to know a beautiful painting.... set a gorgeous table...play with color on your dinner plate...if you clean your closets for Spring, be sure to hang extra hangers for humility, kindness, tenderness, patience, joy, forgiveness, and love. [Colossians 3:12-14]

So, I invite you to leave your winter confines early so that you can watch for signs the next spring you get to greet. Get there first! Allow yourself to be wrapped up in the Spirit's Spring shawl and inhale deeply.

POEMS ABOUT SPRING: [I've shared one already as I introduced this season, but where I've always lived compelled me to add just one more…] I encourage you to read the whole of this lengthy poem!

"Lilacs" —*Amy Lowell*

Lilacs, False blue, White, Purple,
Color of lilac,
Your great puffs of flowers
Are everywhere in this my New England……………………

Lilacs always remind me of being a young Catholic grade-school girl who in May would walk each evening with my best friend, Susan, from our homes to church for the nightly month of Mary devotions. So many people there would have ready-made bouquets of flowers to place in front of Mary's altar, but Sue and I did not have gardens and lamented that we came empty handed. One evening we decided that Mrs. C's abundant lilac bushes that we passed along the way, could certainly afford a few clippings for us to bring so quietly we began to snip off a few branches to make 2 small bouquets to bring to church. Mrs. C came out of her house just then and was quite upset to see us "stealing" her lilacs. We both tearfully pleaded our cause and upon discovering where we were headed with her lilacs, she relented and sent us happily on our way. I think of this event, and Mrs. C, and my buddy Susan who died not so very long ago, every Spring when first I notice that lilacs are back in bloom!

SONGS OF SPRING:

"Here comes the Sun" —*George Harrison*

................Little darling, it's been a long cold lonely winter
Little darling, it feels like years since it's been here
Here comes the sun (doo doo doo)
Here comes the sun, and I say It's all right....................

"April in Paris" —*Yip Harburg*

I never knew the charm of spring;I never met it face to face
I never new my heart could sing
I never missed a warm embrace
Till April in Paris, chestnuts in blossom...........................
"All Hail The Gladsome Easter Morn" —*Anonymous*
il the gladsome Easter morn,
For which the springtime's flow'rs are born;
Earth wears her gayest robes today,
And casts her Lenten garb away.......................................

GREETING SPRING WITH DÉCOR:

Into your prayer space, consider a tiny apple blossom twig, a nest, and/or force a bit of forsythia in a vase of warm water. At your front door, try a simple twig wreath or embroidery hoop with a few scattered spring flowers and a hand-lettered wooden sign tucked in with your very own greeting and nod to the season. If you are obsessed as I am with glass domes of every size and shape, place a potted violet inside a vintage teapot with maybe a lace doily underneath, or be reactive with whatever spells SPRING to YOU! Online sources such as Pinterest are a virtual treasure trove of ideas…go there for inspiration, then put your unique signature on it. Visually show on the outside and inside of your home that internally you have greeted, honored and embraced this marvelous season!

SPRING RECIPES:

Hot Cross Buns

[a recipe in my collection since the dairy that delivered milk to my door when I was a young Mom, printed it in their calendar that year. [1978?] Since then, I have baked countless dozens for our Easter Saturday family Brunch, and delivered to many friends on Good Friday so they could eat them to break their fast come next morning]

Ingredients

2 cups flour
½ cup sugar
4 tsp baking powder
½ tsp each baking soda & salt & cinnamon
6 Tblsp butter
½ cup raisins
1 ¼ cup cottage cheese (small curd)
1 egg
½ tsp vanilla

Directions

Preheat oven to 425 degrees. Combine 1st 6 ingredients up to and including cinnamon. Cut in butter until mixture resembles course meal. Stir in raisins. Combine cottage cheese, egg and vanilla and beat until smooth. Add to flour mixture and mix well, kneading 10 times on floured surface with floured hands! Shape dough into 12 balls and place on dry cookie sheet. Bake for about 18 minutes. Cool and then glaze marking each with a cross.

Glaze: 1 cup confectioners sugar with 2 Tblsp milk and ¼ tsp vanilla.

Source: Sherman's Dairy, Woodstock, CT

Lorette's Frozen Strawberry Pie

[A treasured friend offered this as our dessert one time when we visited long ago. I passed it on to my 3 daughters, and the oldest, Sarah, prepared it for our family every Easter]

Ingredients

2 9" graham cracker crusts
1 10 oz package frozen strawberries (thawed)
1 cup sugar
2 egg whites
1 TB lemon juice
1 cup heavy cream

Directions

Prepare crusts as directed on package. Line the bottom of 2- 9" pie pans or 1- 13" by 9" cake pan with the crust. Put berries, sugar, egg whites and lemon juice in a large bowl. Beat 15 minutes on high speed. Whip heavy cream until peaks form and fold into the berry mixture. Pile high onto crusts. Freeze 2 hours or more. Allow to defrost somewhat to serve.

Afterword

I write this book nearing the end of Summer and nearing the end of my time away in Vermont that I took to be able to do it! I have tried to convey two important thoughts: 1. That the practice of flowing with the rhythm of the four seasons can and will enrich your life and your spiritual longings, and 2. How remarkably simple it is to do!

I must share a strong connection I have with the practice of walking a labyrinth path that so strongly mimics the natural ebb and flow of the four seasons. As a certified labyrinth facilitator, I have often "kept the sacred space" for various groups of all ages as they walk the path. From that posture I have learned much of the labyrinth's restorative possibilities. After introducing folks to basic information about the labyrinth, a facilitator simply sits and gently holds the space while the group walks its twists and turns. It is during that silent, powerful time that I am so often drawn to metaphors that call to mind the natural turning of the seasons. So like the returning cycle of the four seasons, the labyrinth path is one you can count on! Will one season always follow another? Always does!! So too on the winding path there are repeated curves and turns, but putting doubts aside, you've been told that you are headed to the center. Each of the circular trails, even though tempting the walker to suspect they are "off track" at times, surely and slowly brings you to the center. The seasons too sometimes cause you to seriously doubt one will follow another. (This is especially experienced in New England winters that often labor to transition to Spring!) But one can rely on the pattern! Spring WILL follow winter each and every year!

Sometimes too the seasons mimic exactly how one is feeling inwardly, for example Spring might find you ready and awakened to new possibilities and a brand new start. Other years, Spring may indeed come, but for many reasons the deadness and emptiness of Winter persist in our souls not wanting to let go. But if you keep walking, keep leaning into the rhythm of the season upon you, slowly and surely you reach the center of yourself.

Walking the seasons (by honoring each one) and walking a labyrinth is startlingly similar. After staying awhile in gratitude in the center, it is time to walk out following the exact circular path you walked on the way in. This time, your soul seeks how you can give back what the labyrinth has gifted you with. So too, we need to walk out of one season reluctantly sometimes but surely eager to follow where the next one leads. Each one gifts us with so many graces and blessings. In the interior time "between seasons" we ask ourselves: how can I give back and to whom?

If you have never experienced walking a labyrinth, I urge you to find one, preferably with a guide or facilitator. I am certain your walk will be blessed, no matter the season!

The four seasons come and go in our lives in a repeated and dependable rhythm. Often however, we are barely cognizant of their impact let alone grateful for the gifts they potentially give us. They instead mark the passage of time for us only, and sometimes even depressingly cause a strong desire to STOP them, to stop time going by us too quickly while we are caught up in "making a living".

What if we were to rediscover each of these seasons so as to tap into the gifts they wait to give us each and every time they come along? What if we were to learn how to celebrate each season and allow ourselves to be wrapped in the tender mercies each one offers directly from the hand of our good God? This book has been my personal invitation to do just that! I leave you with one more question, and even attempt to answer it. Can greeting and honoring the four seasons make a difference in how we live our lives, grow spiritually, and accept life's difficulties? I believe it can!

In 2008, I was diagnosed with two different strains of breast cancer, one in each breast. The thirteen-month surgery, chemotherapy, radiation process was a challenging time for me and for those who love me. In 2012, I was diagnosed with kidney cancer, a mere four years after breast cancer. Both journeys of surviving this disease were anchored in a spirituality of the seasons! My lowest days would be transformed simply by an intentional and reflective winter ride in the snow, or a new Spring wreath on my front door, sitting outside in the July sunshine, or listening to an October breeze play my backyard chimes. I have yearned for and lived "a seasoned life" for close to 73 years now, and so wish the same for you too!

This book is purely a collection of thoughts and a direct result of decades of personal reflection, and inspiration from many mentors and authors. I give this collection to you, my readers, in the hope they might prompt you to choose to live a more "seasoned" life yourself! May the God of all our seasons bless you most tenderly.

Group Discussion

For those who would like to further engage with the suggestions I've given for 'keeping' the seasons, perhaps with a friend or with a group, here is a possible segue into a group study that includes faith-sharing questions.

Possible questions for discussion:

1. Which season seems to describe you best? Which one do you look forward to the most simply because it embodies your deepest desires and the essence of who you are?

2. In which season is it easiest for you to find God? Why? Does it say anything about you and where you might be on your spiritual journey?

3. Choose one of the following passages from scripture and share with one another a sense you might have that God's vibrant Word truly has something to say about the rhythm of the seasons, and the importance of humans tapping into them to grow spiritually.

   • God spoke: "Lights! Come out! Shine in Heaven's sky! Separate Day from Night. Mark seasons and days and years, Lights in Heaven's sky to give light to Earth." And there it was. [Genesis 1:14-15]

   • For as long as Earth lasts, planting and harvest, cold and heat, Summer and winter, day and night will never stop." [Genesis 8:22]

   • But this people—what a people! Uncontrollable, untamable runaways. It never occurs to them to say, 'How can we honor our God with our lives, The God who gives rain in both spring and autumn and maintains the rhythm of the seasons, Who sets aside time each year for harvest and keeps everything running smoothly for us?' Of course, you don't! Your bad behavior blinds you to all this. Your sins keep my blessings at a distance. [Jeremiah5:23-25]

- To everything there is a season, a time for every purpose under heaven. (Ecclesiastes 3:1)
- I am telling you to open your eyes and take a good look at what's right in front of you. [John 4:35]

_____

SUMMER Words, Poems, and Journaling Questions

cultivate

slow down

relish

REST

go barefoot

linger

The Summer Day --*Mary Oliver*
(Ask a volunteer to read the whole of this
poem aloud and render it with emotion!)

Who made the world?
Who made the swan, and the black bear?
Who made the grasshopper?
This grasshopper, I mean-.......................................
(Most people only know the last 2 lines of Oliver's
poem, "The Summer Day," but they truly miss the
heart of it if they don't hear it all the way through!)

Journaling questions:

How so I plan to rest, relish, linger and slow down this coming
summer?

Which of God's many faces do I hope to discover?

Will I take time apart? When? Where? To do what?

AUTUMN Words, Poems, and Journaling Questions

Autumn words to break open:
Gather in/let go!
Reckon
Mature
Trust
Melancholy/exhilarating
Begin again

Journaling questions:

1. How can I get out of my own way and let God's Spirit take charge of my life?
2. In what ways could I stir within my children, grandchildren, nieces, nephews, or neighbors' children to pass on to them what I have learned of God's Spirit?
3. Is there a "goodbye" in my life right now that I am reluctant to make?

plunge
down

lie fallow

hibernate

be in solitude

reflect

wait

To a Wreath of Snow Emily Brontë
(Once again, please do look up and read the
whole of this lovely ode to snow!)

O transient voyager of heaven!
O silent sign of winter skies!
What adverse wind thy sail has driven
To dungeons where a prisoner lies?............

<u>Journaling Questions</u>:

1. In dark times, how easily can you find deep within you that which is still alive and full of hope?
2. How do you respond to silence and solitude? Do you know why?
3. Is it easy or difficult for you to sit still, "lie fallow," just Be? If it is easy, how do you use time to be still? If it is difficult, what steps could you take to slowly learn the value of taking time to "not do," but to just be?

SPRING Words, Poems, and Journaling Questions

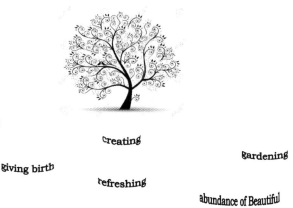

becoming

creating

gardening

giving birth

refreshing

abundance of Beautiful

Metamorphosis (Be sure to read it all...) --May Sarton

Always it happens when we are not there —
The tree leaps up alive in the air,
Small open parasols of Chinese green
Wave on each twig. But who has ever seen.....................

Journaling question:

Does this season often catch me unaware? What prevents me from taking it all in? Is it my work? This is the same season of Easter vigils, First Communions, and registrations for next year???

How can I be the face of God to others if I don't fall in love with that Face each time it manifests itself anew every new season?

How can I notice more? How can I show up more often?

Printed in the United States
by Baker & Taylor Publisher Services